What are we feckin' like?

THE BOOK of IRISH CHARACTERS

First published 2007 by The O'Brien Press Ltd.
12 Terenure Road East, Rathgar, Dublin 6, Ireland.
Tel: +353 1 4923333; Fax: +353 1 4922777
E-mail: books@obrien.ie
Website: www.obrien.ie
ISBN: 978-1-84717-060-6

British Library Cataloguing-in-Publication Data
Murphy, Colin
Jaysus, what are we like?: the book of feckin' Irish characters.-
(Feckin' series)
1. National characteristics, Irish - Miscellanea 2.
National characteristics, Irish - Humor 3. Ireland - Social life
and customs - Miscellanea 4. Ireland -
Social life and customs - Humor
I. Title II. O'Dea, Donal
941.5'0824
1 2 3 4 5 6 7 8 9 10
07 08 09 10 11 12

Printed by Graspo CZ, a.s.

Czech Republic

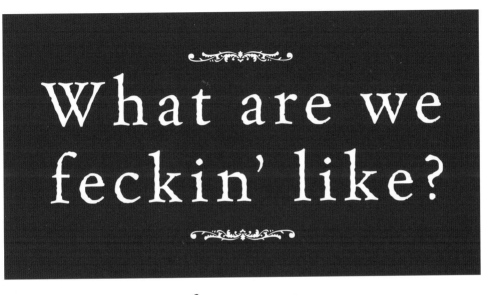

What are we feckin' like?

THE BOOK *of* IRISH CHARACTERS

COLIN MURPHY & DONAL O'DEA

THE O'BRIEN PRESS
DUBLIN

The Feckin' Collection

B & B Landlady

Although they're a vanishing breed now, up to a decade ago, the traditional B & B landlady was one of God's warriors in the last line of defence against illicit hanky panky between unwed couples. Assuming the role of the surrogate Irish Mammy, the nosey oul' bag would listen at walls and doors for the telltale sound of the headboard banging against the wall or the bedsprings creaking like a kangaroo was using the bed as a trampoline. And, by God, if you were caught, you'd be ejected in the morning before you'd even got your black pudding. Nowadays of course the Irish landlady has completely changed. So much so that some of them will actually hand you a black pudding on your way into the bedroom.

VIRGIN HOUSE
B&B
NO VACANCIES
NO SNEAKING
INTO EACH OTHERS
ROOM FOR SEX

Bank Manager

God be with the days when the average bank manager was one of the local gentry – a jovial, red-faced, plump figure who knew everyone by name and was treated with great respect altogether. Your modern Irish bank manager, on the other hand, thinks like a heroin dealer and the drug he/she doles out is money. See, they get you hooked by handing it over like they can't wait to be rid of it. 'Hi, I need money to build a waterslide

> o BANK OF EIRE o
> "We own you suckers"
> o   o

from my bathroom into my duckpond?' No problem! 'Hi, I'd like to buy shares in a pasta farm.' Here you go! 'Hi, I'd like to convert the garage on my 3 bed semi-d into a riding stable.' Absolutely! And just like a drug, the more you get, the more you have to have. Only problem is, now he has you hooked for life. What a complete banker!

Barman

Nowadays, with the smoking ban, Ireland's pubs are smoke free. Unfortunately, most of them are also customer free. But in bygone days (about three years ago), the Irish barman was truly legendary in his ability to single-handedly serve hordes of insatiable customers while simultaneously sympathising with the lone depressed drinker, singing along with the rowdy  mob, stopping a bottle fight while making an Irish coffee, writing the entire works of Brendan Behan on the head of a pint of Guinness, giving directions to passing tourists looking for their ancestors and telling a dirty joke about a girl using her 36 D-cup bra to make a particular cocktail. Buy that man a drink.

9

Bride

What's the most important thing to an Irish bride-to-be? Love? Security? Family?

No, it's the opportunity to aimlessly blow a fortune on a Cecil B DeMille-scale wedding in which she's the tyrannical star and the hundreds of green-with-envy guests fall in praise at her feet! Actually, it's more likely they'll be green with nausea  at the hideous levels of tackiness: doves being released, bride arriving at church by chopper, peacocks wandering around the hotel lawn, peacocks arriving at hotel by chopper ... the more tasteless the more the Irish bride must have it. At least the white dress seems to have survived. Which is strange, considering that most Irish brides are as pure as the driven slush.

Big Thick Culchie

The image of the big thick culchie is that of a big, red-faced galoot who is such a gobdaw he or she thinks farm is spelt E-I-E-I-O. The males have a propensity for drinking twenty pints a day and yelling 'yee haa', and dress in old sweaters that have more holes than wool and mucky old pants tucked into wellies. The female culchie drinks and dresses with equal sophistication and also has hairy legs and armpits, and child-bearing hips so big she looks capable of having a hurling team all at one go. Of course, this image of people from the country-side is a myth – female culchies shave their armpits nowadays.

BMW Driver

Fine piece of engineering, the BMW. Sadly, the people who drive them mostly seem like a failed experiment in genetic engineering. It's not commonly known that Irish BMW drivers undergo a separate test from all other car drivers. To be successful, you must break as many red lights as possible in the shortest possible time, break every Irish speed limit, and,

| BMW DRIVER |
| RULES OF THE ROAD |
| I: GO FAST. 2: ALL PEOPLE MUST DIE. |

if you're lucky, break a few pedestrians'/cyclists' bones. There is also a psychological assessment to see if you're a big enough arrogant bollix or wagon. All that being ok, you're granted your licence to pose with your ganky taste in music blaring out of your open window, in case people aren't looking at you enough. Every two years, however, BMW drivers must undergo the NCOT test, otherwise known as the National Cop-On Test. There is an extremely high failure rate.

Grafton Street
Boutique Shopper

To qualify as a bona fide Grafton Street shopper you must have one of the following: a rich daddy, a rich hubby, a winning lotto ticket or the now familiar combination of a credit card and absolutely no brain. Sadly, this last species of GS shoppers form by far the largest grouping and can be identified in Grafton Street as they emerge from their foraging by

WE ACCEPT:

VISA

DINERS

GOBSHITES

RICH EEJITS

SPENDTHRIFTS

the fact that they are practically clattering you on the side of the feckin' head with their logoed bags to make sure you know where they've been.

Cailín

Ah, the famed Irish cailín of old. What a sight to behold. And sure don't they deserve our admiration for their purity – going to mass every Sunday, confession every Friday, dancin' jigs at the crossroads in traditional costumes, which was all the more amazing considering they were also wearin' padlocked, reinforced steel knickers, two inches thick, that required a blow torch to remove. Will we ever see her like again? Let's feckin' hope not.

CAILÍN LINGERIE "MADE FROM GIRDERS"

Céilí Dancer

Becoming skilled as an Irish céilí dancer requires many years' training – usually from about the age of six. Alternatively, it requires about eight pints and to be completely gee-eyed.

CÉILÍ DANCE TONIGHT IN VILLAGE HALL (Only First 10,000 admitted)

Generally speaking, traditional céilí dancers are very jolly and energetic young wans and young fellas, capable of hopping about on one foot for seventeen hours, non-stop, and capable of touching their nose with their kneecap forty times a minute. And you simply have to admire anyone who can make sense of a dance that can involve either two people roaring 'Gerrup-ye-boy-ye!' or 235,983 people roaring 'Gerrup-ye-boy-ye!'

Celtic Tiger

Twenty- to thirty-something, Mr Dynamic, works ridiculously long hours and insists he loves it, eats his breakfast in car on M50 – energy bar made from cereal factory floor sweepings.

Often eats lunch in car on M50 as still stuck there since breakfast. Lunch consists of tiny plastic container of liquidised concentrated vegetables and bird droppings and costs the same as a sack of potatoes, twelve turnips, ten tomatoes and a field of parsnips. Drinks hard after work, snorts cocaine, flashes loadsa cash at pissed skangers in nightclubs. Goes to gym at weekends so he can pay someone €800 a year for the privilege of running 5km on a treadmill, which, ironically, is a metaphor for his life: going nowhere fast.

Celtic Tigress

Similar eating, drinking, drug addictions and driving habits to Celtic Tiger (see previous page). Tough as nails, immaculately turned out in stupidly expensive clothes and is so sexually liberated that her experiences would make a Ladd Lane brasser blush. Loves to arrange 'power breakfast meetings' at 7.30am to show her dedication, at which her half-asleep colleagues merely consider her a dedicated geebag.

Makes sure everyone knows she has regular shopping weekends in New York, where she shops in the same global chains you'll find in Grafton Street. Burns wick at both ends and manages to get on everyone else's.

BITCH RED LIPSTICK

Chip Shop Owner

Think of Italian cuisine ... ah, veal scallopine ... mussels marinara ... risotto al quattro formaggi ... and, hang on ... feckin' chips??? How, in the name of Jaysus, did Italians in Ireland ever become associated with the most unsophisticated food  on the planet? Everywhere else in the world they open pizzerias and the like. In Ireland, they came, they saw and they started deep frying battered sausages and onion rings. Anyway, the owner. You know the guy – his name is Luigi. Or Mario. Or Dario. Remember him? You've only ever seen him when you're in rag order after ten pints. He's got olive skin, big dark eyes and when he says those magic words: 'Your batter burger and chips are ready!'... well, you simply want to fall on your knees and kiss his feet in admiration.

Civil Servant

Since the dark day back in the Seventies when Jack Lynch decided to win the election by hiring three-quarters of the entire adult population into the civil service, Irish civil servants have developed a level of inactivity unique on the planet. Rule 1 of the job is never to answer the phone. Of course, it might be Mary from upstairs wanting a break from scratching her arse all day, so occasionally you *have* to answer. Rule 2. If you get a member of the public, put him/her on hold just long enough to go away for a midweek break in Budapest. When you do get back to him/her, transfer him/her to the wrong department. If each department obeys this rule, Joe Public never gets anywhere and nothing gets done, which, as you learn on your first day, is the entire purpose of the Irish Civil Service.

Corrupt Politician

(See also Cute Hoor)

You find these the world over, of course, but in Ireland the two words seem to go together as naturally as strawberries and cream. Of course they tell us that those days are gone. Today's Dáil member is a pillar of integrity and a tower of fortitude. Yeah, right. Sadly, many aspiring TDs see the Dáil as a means of getting a foot on the beanstalk and haven't actually got a clue about politics. The fact is, a lot of them still think passing a Green Paper is some form of cash pay-off, that a Dáil Session means everyone goes on the lash with some rich builders, and that the Genetically Modified Food Bill is the slip of paper you get in a posh restaurant and then doctor it to claim more expenses.

100
BROWN
ENVELOPES
(EXTRA LARGE)

Courier

The Irish courier's motorcycle is specially designed with a speedometer that starts at 50kph and has no upper limit. You may witness the effects of this by observing a courier as he takes off. The moment he gets on the bike, he shoots down the road like he's been propelled by a giant, invisible elastic band. The courier's unique bike design also allows him, incredibly, to pass though solid objects, like pedestrians or cyclists. While the courier remains unaffected by this amazing matter displacement, unfortunately the result for the person he encounters is that they are splattered across a nearby wall in small pieces.

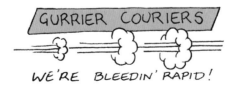

Celebrity Criminal

The key to star status in the Irish criminal underworld is not ruthlessness or cunning or leadership, it's finding a catchy nickname that the tabloids can have some wordplay with. For example, 'The General Outflanks the Gardaí again'. Your nickname can reflect your animal instincts (The Viper), or your perceived lifestyle (The Monk), but it should always be colourful and snappy. Rumour has it that among the hopefuls who didn't quite make it to the criminal fraternity were those who chose the following nicknames: The Undercover Guard, The Big-Mouthed Gobshite and the Lesser-Spotted Tit Warbler.

Cute Hoor

(See also Corrupt Politician)

Though not all cute hoors are politicians, the reverse is usually true. But whether a TD, a businessman, the local priest or publican, Ireland has a vast population of this particular species. Every little village or town possesses at least one. You

> **TAX RETURN**
>
> OCCUPATION: *Cute hoor*
> ADDRESS: *Yacht in Caribbean*
> INCOME: *Zilch*

know the guy, he's usually over-weight from dining and drinking on your money, he's got a hearty handshake and a great big smile in the middle of a great big red face, he puts on the poor mouth something awful, he's everyone's best friend and he'd happily shite in your parlour and charge you for the privilege. To be avoided like Boris Yeltsin avoided sobriety.

Cyclist

Now, cyclists are probably all lovely lads and lasses normally, but once they throw the leg over that contraption and hit the streets, they turn into a bunch of wojusly arrogant bowsies as ignorant as a sack of arses. An Irish cyclist will scream abuse at a pedestrian for not using the zebra crossing, then cheerfully plough through a red light, mount the pavement, ride on the wrong side of the road at night with no lights, scrape the paint off a car, kick a couple of rubbish bins aside, knock over an old lady, then pull out a Kalashnikov and kill twenty people. (OK, the last one's a slight exaggeration.) And they're so feckin' self-righteous! They say we all spring from apes. Cyclists didn't spring far enough.

Da

If you're a modern-day father and you think you have it hard, spare a thought for your own Da and remember the trials he went through to 'rare' you. Worked 246 hours a week, had to walk thirty-two miles to work in the rain every morning and it was uphill there and back, only having a raw potato to eat all day. Was paid 2s/6d, three-quarters of which went on tax. After giving your sainted Mammy her cut, he'd only have a single penny left to buy a pint. And here's where you'd have to admire his economic adroitness: he managed to get gee-eyed five nights a week on that single old penny.

Devout Catholic

There was a time when we were all devout Catholics in Ireland (except for the 12 Protestants, 4 Jews, 2 Moslems and the Hindi). You think getting a seat at the World Cup Final is hard? Try getting a seat at Sunday mass in Ireland thirty years ago! You wouldn't have a hope! Standing room only. Most of them are gone now – either dead or converted to atheism. But a few still remain, ready and willing to be judgemental about you. You'll be able to recognise them because they believe the following to be sins: sex, alcohol, sex, swearing, sex, divorce, sex, breathing, sex, eating, sex, sleeping, sex. Devout Catholics are also opposed to sex.

43

Dirty Dubliner

Unjustified stereotypical images can, unfortunately, build up about certain groups, like the Drunken Paddy, the Tight-Fisted Scot, the Humourless German. In the case of the Dirty Dubliner, the image is utterly, 100% justified. Dubliners are filthy. They love to wallow in their own muck. They regard it  as their absolute right to litter the streets of Dublin – many actually regard it as their duty. If they see a clean, unspoilt corner in a park or by a canal they will actually set off for the nearest shop to buy something in a plastic container, not because they're hungry or thirsty, but with the sole intent of making the clean spot filthy enough for them to feel comfortable in. Kerry may have the most All-Ireland titles, but in the manky dirty stakes, Dublin is out of sight.

45

Female Binge Drinker

One of our more modern characters in Ireland, the female binge drinker does for the image of Ireland what Eamon Casey did for the Catholic Church. She can be seen most nights in the centre of any town or city, staggering around footless with a mini-skirt halfway up her arse and a brightly coloured boob tube which has been decorated with a dollop of her own puke. Becomes ossified very quickly on shorts – the booze giving her the illusion of being attractive to men. Can't comprehend why the only two things that keep attracting each other are her head and the floor.

47

First Communicant

In the old days, your parents scrimped hard to get the money together to buy you a little suit or a white dress for your First Communion. Now that we're all (supposedly) Mr & Mrs Loadsa Euros, it seems our levels of taste have declined in parallel with our poverty. The modern day Irish Catholic parent (who, incidentally, doesn't believe in God) uses his/her child's First Communion as a means of showing off how loaded he/she is, by dressing their unfortunate ten-year-old First Communicant in things like tails, all-white suits, braces, pocket watches, monacles and top hats – and that's just the girls.

49

GAA Diehard

This head-the-ball will blather you into your grave with arguments about how Gaelic football and hurling are much tougher sports than soccer or rugby. He can name every All-Ireland winner since the shaggin' dinosaurs walked the earth and he has been to every GAA ground in the country in all weathers, thereby proving that not only is he committed, but also that he should be.

He is most likely a republican with a dislike of Brits and will bore the arse off you about the disgrace of the hallowed ground of Croker being opened to these 'foreign' games. He is also likely to be the gobshite spotted at the Ireland-England rugby match holding up a 'No Foreign Games' sign while wearing a Celtic shirt.

Gaeilgeoir

(Gaelic Language Enthusiast)

You studied Irish for fourteen years, but when you finished school your Irish was completely wojus. How? Well, blame this guy. He's the one who insisted on the antiquated teaching methods and the tortuous slog through *Peig*. The reason for this is that he secretly wants the number of Irish speakers to dwindle, making him feel even more elitist and superior. He has a name like Aonghus Muirgheas Mac an Bhreitheamhan or something and probably has a long shaggy beard. In fact, so do his wife and children. He won't converse in anything but Irish, so nobody talks to him except other Gaeilgeoirs, which is fine with everyone else, who would only have three little words to say to him for the shite he put them through in school: Póg mo hole.

Gurrier

Gurriers in general are a doddle to recognise nowadays, dressed in their uniform of a hoodie – usually white in colour. One advantage of the hoodie is that when the gurrier robs a shop or something, the guards issue a description which narrows the possible suspect list to 249,371. It also has the advantage of hiding the mass of whiteheads, blackheads and shiny red spots grappling with each other to be the first to explode onto the gurrier's face. As a rule, gurriers mate with skangers behind skips before setting them on fire. The skip, that is, not the skanger.

HOOD

55

Irish Holidaymaker on the Med

It's easy to spot these, as the locals generally have an attractive olive complexion, whereas the Irish holidaymaker will appear to have flesh that's been drained of all red blood cells, soaked in bleach, then given a coat of whitewash. This will change after two days in the sun so that it appears the resort has been invaded by a species of giant mutant lobsters. The male of this species will often wear a thong by the pool, which can cause bouts of severe vomiting in other residents. The female wears only the bottom half of a string bikini, exposing hideous rippling cheeks and ganky, pumpkin-like boobs. People have been known to suffer from post-traumatic stress disorder after exposure.

Local Garda Sergeant

Less of a recognisable figure in Ireland's larger cities, but in your sleepy little town, by God, here's a man you don't want to cross. He's usually six feet six inches tall (or is that wide?) and has a very large purplish head, which is, luckily, supported by three chins. He rules his domain with a fist of steel with which he will mercilessly crush any criminal masterminds, like someone who parks on a yellow line, has a sip of drink one second after hours, or doesn't wheel their bin in off the footpath. Has nothing to do all day except give the evil eye to teenagers in hoodies. Favourite expression: 'Go ahead, make my day, give me two more doughnuts with my latte.'

59

RIGHT! IT'S TIME TO GIVE HOGAN THE GOOD COP BAD COP ROUTINE.
BUT SARGE, HE ONLY CAME IN FOR A PASSPORT APPLICATION FORM.
GARDA

Male Binge Drinker

As equally pathetic as his female counterpart, the male binge drinker wanders the streets of modern Ireland thinking he's the funniest thing since sliced bread. And since sliced bread wasn't funny to start with, this makes him particularly nauseating. He has to have at least ten drinks before he has the balls to approach a 'mot', which is unfortunate, because by then his balls don't work any more. He compensates for  his failure with women by roaring at the top of his voice to attract the attention of passers-by, who he rewards with the spectacle of him having a slash in his own pants or sending a jet of projectile vomit down his best friend's back. Age profile: 18–25. Mental age profile: 12.

Mammy

One of the most recognisable of all Irish characters is the beloved (esp. of men) Irish Mammy. Who else would be bringing them their cornflakes with warm milk in bed when they're in their thirties? Who else would scrub the unthinkable off their jocks with one hand while ironing their socks with the other, and without a word of complaint? Who else would collect them from the Garda station at 3am, listen to their drunken ramblings, and then tuck them into bed with the promise in the morning of a sausage and bacon sambo on sliced batch loaf with plenty of butter? And who else would defend them to the hilt despite minor shortcomings like being arrested for head-butting an old lady and stealing her pension to buy dope? Ah, the Irish Mammy. She's the mother of all mammies.

Middle Class Protestant

In the old days most Irish Catholic people had a totally unambiguous attitude towards southern Irish Prods – complete and utter jealousy. Not only were the jammy hoors all loaded, thanks to their evil Brit ancestors raping and pillaging of our fair land (at least that's what the Christian Brothers taught us), but on top of that they didn't HAVE to go to mass on Sunday! We've all sort of blended together nowadays with equal amounts of dosh and indifference to God, so the only way to tell an Irish Protestant is by the name. The chances are, for example, that anyone called Nigel Ramsbottom-Blythe wasn't at the Pope's mass in the Phoenix Park in 1979.

Millionaire/Billionaire

Ireland has these by the thousand these days, by the hundred thousand even, at least on paper. Thanks to the illusion created by a bottomless pit of bank credit and the property 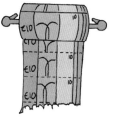 boom, all our homes are worth trillions, and if we were all to sell up tomorrow we'd all be able to retire to the Caribbean and destroy their country instead. We actually also have a sizeable number of billionaires in Ireland and, by Jaysus, they're determined to hang on to their billions. None of that oul' benefactor shite for our lads. Build a ward for sick children? Go and ask me bollox! Open a park? Go and shite! Sponsor the local hurling team? Go and ask me hole! The only consolation is that it's an awful lot of cash thay can go and shove up their collective arses.

Moore Street Trader

Most people in Ireland could probably be described as speaking English with a touch of accent. On Dublin's Moore Street, the traders speak Accent with a touch of English.

'Get yer mackril, tree for fiev youros'

(Get your mackerel, three for five euro).

'Fier lierers, ate forreh youro tirtie'

(Fire lighters, eight for a euro thirty).

CHICKENS GOIN' CHEAP CHEAP

'Why-end-up ty moror boikes ony nien nientie nien'

(Wind-up toy motor bikes only nine ninety-nine).

And a trip to Moore Street wouldn't be complete without a little bit of that cutting wit:

'Dat carra's norra mickey, missis – it's not goin' to gerrany biggar by feelin' ih! *(That carrot's not a penis, madam – it's not going to get any bigger by feeling it).*

Mr Church
Money Collector

He stands at the end of your pew, grim-faced; piercing, accusing eyes fixed on you as the wooden church collection plate is passed inexorably in your direction. He's been doing this for thirty years and he knows all the tricks, like making a fist to surreptitiously drop a mere few coppers into the plate. But the light tinkle of your piteous donation betrays you and now there's no escaping the steeliness of his eyes boring holes in your head, silently calling you a manky, scabby oul' bowsie. And when he passes the priest, there's a brief exchange and the priest glances your way, vengeance writ across his face, and you know the next time you go to confession the penance is just going to be feckin' brutal!

Traditional Musician

To qualify as one of these you have to be able to play a fiddle, an accordion, a concertina, a banjo, a bodhrán, a tin whistle, a mandolin, a flute, a harmonica and the spoons – though not all at the same time. Like your close relative, the céilí dancer, you also have to be able simultaneously to yell 'gowanyeboyye!' while you play, which can be a bit of a pain in the hole if you're trying to play a tin whistle at the time. You also have to frown at anyone in the pub who's not giving you their complete and undivided attention, and absolutely scowl at any fecker who dares to speak a word during a rendition of that timeless classic, 'diddleee-eidel-diedle-di'.

Northside Mot

Having a 'mot' (girlfriend, for the uninitiated) from Dublin's northside can be best summed up by the following story: A northside mot is in the post office, filling out a child benefit form. The woman behind the counter asks for her kids' names.

'Deco, Deco, Deco, Deco, Deco, Deco, Deco, Deco, Deco and Deco,' she replies.

EAU DE
DONAGHMEDE
€1.99

Amazed, the assistant asks: 'And what if you want to call one of them into the house for something. Won't they all come running?'

The northside youngwan looks at the assistant as if she's as thick as a heifer's arse.

'Course not, I'd use his surname.'

Parking Attendant

One of those venerable old characters from Dublin in the rare oul' times and now rapidly disappearing. Thanks be to Jaysus! The parking attendant had a strict uniform code of a peaked cap to impart authority, and every other stitch in rag order, to give the impression that he was a few onions short of a stew.

He'd stand behind your car, going, 'Keep comin', bud. Yer grand ... yer grand ... yer grand ...' until you'd hear your brake light shattering against a lamp post, at which point he'd yell, 'hold it there!' You'd then be obliged to give him 'a few bob' to keep an eye on your car, in case some bollix smashed your windscreen – him.

Priest

Many people would find it hard to believe the place formerly occupied by the priest in Irish society. Obedience and reverence towards Father Whateverhisname was almost religious. His position is best summed up by the story of the two oul' wans living across from the brothel. A rabbi goes in and they 'tut-tut' in disgust. A Protestant minister goes in and they are revolted. 'Typical,' they mutter. The local Catholic priest goes in, and one says to the other: 'Sure, one of the poor girls must be very sick.'

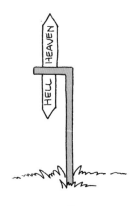

Publican

There was a time when publicans in Ireland actually outnumbered customers, or at least it seemed that way. So perhaps it was inevitable that their numbers would dwindle. And, of course, for most it's a terribly hard life, having to moan non-stop about overheads and how it hurts them so to keep upping their prices. And imagine the state not organising buses to ferry people to and from their pubs so they could spend loadsa money getting utterly gee-eyed? And why don't people understand that the reason two half pints costs a bleedin' fortune compared to a pint is all the extra labour involved in pulling them?

Lads, will yis ever go and ask me arse.

Punter

The famous Irish-American pool player, Danny McGoorty, once said that the first time he backed a horse was the unluckiest day of his life – it won. Similarly unlucky punters can be found in your local bookies any time of the working day, filling out betting slips with names like The Emperor's Runners, Lightning Pants or The Princess's Knickers. They usually have a red face caused by their heads being bent over the *Star* racing pages all day, and they have two expressions – a) Big smile: I won! I'm bleedin' savage at picking the winners and I'm going to get scuttered. b) Grim-faced despair: Shite, I just blew the week's shopping money; maybe I shouldn't have picked a horse called SloMo Sleepy Shoes.

BETTER
BOOKIES

€100 to
win on
Tortoise
feet.

Returned Emigrant

There was only one sight worse than watching our best and brightest depart our shores in search of work during the dark days of mass emigration. And that was seeing them come back. Nothing would give you a bigger pain in the arse than having to listen to one of them blathering on about how the USA has this, that and the bleedin' other. Why doesn't Cork or Galway or Dublin have such and such a poxy thing like they do in London? Or, the weather here is brutal compared to Australia. And what made it worse was that they were right! There was mass unemployment, wojus planning, crap infrastructure, rampant corruption. It's different now, of course. The mass unemployment is gone.

Stereotypical Hollywood Irishman

Americans are comfortable with their vague mental image of what other peoples are like and they don't want any of your goddam realism, thanks very much. Which is why Hollywood deals in stereotypes. So much so that they usually employ American 'dialogue coaches' when shooting a movie in Ireland – to teach the locals how to speak with an Irish accent! Which is why we will continue to hear lines like, 'Well, Holy Mary, Mother of God, me bucko, 'tis a fine soft day to be sure to be sure to be sure, and top of the mornin' te ye, begorrah and begob at all at all at all.' Ah, Americans, you gotta love them.

Supporter Da
on the Sideline

You can see him any weekend in your local park – passionate, obsessive, screaming things like, 'Skin 'im, Anto' or 'Mind your house, Seamo!' or 'Get stuck into the little bollix!' And that's just the under-sevens. It's a strange phenomenon — at the sight of their kid playing soccer, normally quiet dads are transformed into lunatics with a thirst for blood. To satisfy this thirst, his offspring has to obey strategic instructions, like, 'Give that gobshite in goal a root in the hole!' He also has to learn quickly to interpret phrases like, 'Dribble down the wing, then dummy the left back with a one-two with head-the-ball.' A clue to these dads' motivations can be found in the oft-heard phrase: 'If the chief scout for Man United doesn't sign you for fifty grand a week, ye can forget about gettin' ice-cream after the game, you useless little fecker.'

WATCH YER FECKIN' HOUSE!!!

Tradesman

Since the dawn of the Celtic Tiger, the language used by Irish tradesmen has undergone a complete transformation. To help understand modern trades' jargon, please refer to the following key phrases/translations:

'I'll be there at 9 on Monday /*I'll be there at 3 on Thursday to scratch me hole for an hour.*'

'Just going for a cuppa, back in 5 minutes/*I'm off to the pub to get scuttered for the afternoon.*'

'I'll have the job done by 5 this evening/*I'll have the job half-done the Christmas after next.*'

'That's not a supporting wall/*I'll be long gone with your dosh when the roof crushes you to death.*'

Volunteer Singer at Wedding

He's the oul' lad who modestly refuses to get up and sing at the wedding until eventually he's so plastered he thinks he's singing to himself in the bath. He stands there, swaying gently on the edge of the stage, mike in one hand, half-pint in the other and launches into Nat King Cole's 'Unforgettable'. It comes out 'Unfurgerrribelllll ... daz waz yooo arrrr ... unfurgerrribellll'. At this point he pauses for a sip, forgets what he's singing and resumes with Bing Crosby's 'White Christmas', even though it's the middle of July. And absolutely no matter what song on the planet he's singing, even if it's the Ukrainian national anthem, it will always, ALWAYS, end with the words: ... 'Eyeeeeee luvvvvvvv youuuuuuuu'.

Writer

We regard ourselves as a nation of great writers, much the way the French regard themselves as a nation of great lovers (we got the short straw). Many of us strive to follow in the footsteps of the Joyces, the Shaws, the Yeatses, weaving words like ... *Tread softly in the Anna Ob-Liviousness of the bee-bottle glade's golden appleicious sun arising on the bewattled clay pigeon ...*

Instead, most of us simply end up weaving words like, *'Go and ask me bollix, ye big dozy shower of muck savages.'*

 COLIN MURPHY is the co-author of the Feckin' series of books on different aspects of Irish culture. He is eminently qualified to write a book on Irish characters as he is the embodiment of many classic Irish characteristics, like deviousness, begrudgery, intemperance, miserliness and general gankiness. When he's not writing these books, he is the Joint Creative Director of one of Ireland's leading advertising agencies, Owens DDB. He is married with two expensive teenagers.

 DONAL O'DEA is also the co-author of the Feckin' series and is of very dubious character himself. His qualifications for working on this book were that he claimed to have the inside track on our race's idiosyncrasies. Unfortunately, it turned out that Idiosyncrasies was a greyhound and the race was the 8.30 at Harold's Cross. He too is the Joint Creative Director of Owens DDB and hopes to get a pay rise for having given them a second plug. He is married with three noisy children and manages the local kids' football team, who've just been relegated to the newly formed 27th division.